HÉCTOR RUIZ MARTÍN

LEARNING TO LEARN

BY KNOWING YOUR BRAIN

A GUIDE FOR STUDENTS

JOHN CATT
FROM HODDER EDUCATION

Orders: please contact Hachette UK Distribution, Hely Hutchinson Centre, Milton Road, Didcot, Oxfordshire, OX11 7HH. Telephone: +44 (0)1235 827827. Email education@hachette.co.uk. Lines are open from 9 a.m. to 5 p.m., Monday to Friday.

ISBN: 9781036005047

© Héctor Ruiz Martín 2023

First published in 2023 by
John Catt from Hodder Education,
An Hachette UK Company
15 Riduna Park, Station Road,
Melton, Woodbridge IP12 1QT
Telephone: +44 (0)1394 389850
www.johncatt.com

MIX
Paper | Supporting responsible forestry
FSC
www.fsc.org
FSC™ C104740

Contents

Why is learning to learn so important?

Whether you are one of those people who think that studying is not your thing or one of those who is not all that bad at it, this book can help you much more than you might think.

My name is Héctor R. Martín and I am a scientist who investigates how the brain works when it is learning. If you give me a chance, I will show you how to make the best out of the effort you put in when you study. Follow my advice and you will soon find out that I'm not bluffing. Maybe what I'll show you will seem like magic to you, but it is just science. Science has helped us figure out the kinds of actions and circumstances that make our brain better remember what it learns.

PROMOTING LEARNING

I'm sure you have noticed that your memory does not work at will. From everything you experience, you cannot decide what you will remember and what you will forget. That is why, when you study, you underline, reread, and repeat chunks of text thinking that these actions will help you remember what you are studying. However, nothing can guarantee that you will remember it. Even if you have a very good memory, it may have let you down on occasion.

That's where I can help you. Because I can tell you about the actions and situations that help your brain to better remember what you study. It doesn't matter if you have a good or bad memory. Either way, these learning strategies will give you an advantage. And if it turns out that you already apply some of them, then I'm sure you will be happy to know that you have found the best formulas. Are you curious?

LEARNING IS A MATTER OF TECHNIQUE

You might be surprised to know that effective learning is more a matter of technique than a natural ability. But it's true: what you do when you study and the way you organize yourself is what really makes the difference. While it is true that some people are better than others at remembering what they learn, learning strategies can help us overcome these differences. Also, as things get more challenging in higher grades, your natural ability often falls short if you don't have good learning strategies.

Let me draw an analogy. Imagine there's a kid who was born with such an unusual physique that she has a natural edge over the other kids when swimming: big hands, strong arms, a broad back, and so on. Now let's say she has never taken any swimming lessons, but we ask her to try to swim from one end of the pool to the other. That person is likely to develop an inefficient swimming style (for example, a dog paddle). But with her excellent physical qualities, she will probably succeed in swimming across the pool using this technique.

Now think of a person who does not have the same physical qualities for swimming, but who has been taught to swim front crawl style (the most effective style). Without a doubt, this person will swim much faster than the other swimmer. Besides, through this technique, she will become a better swimmer because she will develop better physical qualities, such as bigger muscles.

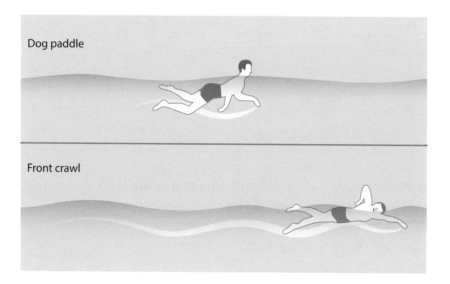

Dog paddle

Front crawl

In this way, learning is a lot like swimming. Some of the learning strategies and techniques we develop are better than others, but they all make a big difference. It doesn't matter how skilled you think you are at learning. Good strategies and techniques will allow you to do much better no matter what level you are at right now.

In fact, as it happens with swimming, having good learning strategies will also improve your qualities as a student in the long term.

Memory gets stronger as you gain knowledge, and good strategies are the most effective way of gaining knowledge and making it last. Your brain changes when you learn things.

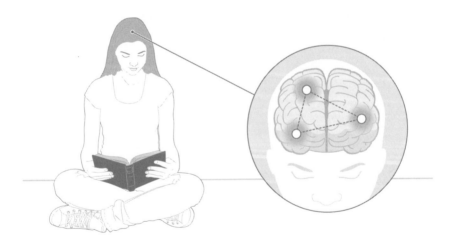

In this book you will discover the keys to how we learn according to science. Learning these keys will help you learn better.

However, I should warn you first...

YOUR PREFERRED METHOD MAY NOT BE THE MOST EFFECTIVE

Students often mistake the way they like to study with the method that will give them the best results. Also, they often delude themselves into thinking that their brain is different and it therefore learns better in a particular way (the one they like). While it is true that all brains are unique, they are not in this respect. The mechanisms that the brain uses to learn are the same for all of us, as are the mechanisms it uses to see, for example. The main differences between us are in our starting point, in our initial skill, which depends on our previous experiences and natural traits. From there, strategies for making progress in learning and improving our skills are based on the same principles. These are the principles of how the brain learns.

So, keep this in mind: eating what we like and eating what is actually good for us are two completely different things. You may like studying in a certain way, but that does not mean that it is the most effective way. Are you interested in knowing how to get the best out of your extraordinary brain?

Whatever your answer, let me tell you the stories of two students who discovered the value of learning to learn.

$\longrightarrow$

When I first met Pablo, he was a frustrated student. Despite trying his hardest, he did not do well in school, and he was particularly bad at math. He was convinced he was not cut out for it.

Although it was not easy at first, Pablo agreed to use some of my tips on how to better deal with school assignments and exams. The first thing he understood was that putting in an effort is not enough. You have to know how to invest that effort productively. And that's when good learning strategies come into play.

It took Pablo some time to adjust to the methods I taught him, but he soon began to see he was improving considerably. After a few months, Pablo's grades were good, something that would have seemed impossible before.

Now Pablo has a degree in physics and is pursuing a doctorate in thermodynamics.

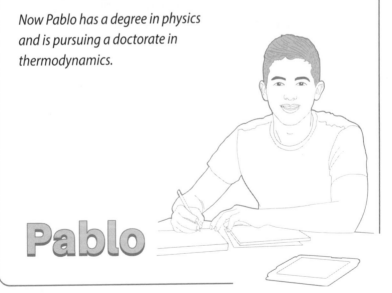

Pablo

Claire was a high school student who had always had very good grades in all school subjects. However, she was feeling sad and disappointed. As much as she kept trying as she always had, she was not getting the same results as before, and she could not understand why. She was beginning to think that she did not have it in her anymore, or that she was not as good as she had thought.

I had a hard time making Claire see that the ability to learn is not so much about having a gift as it is about having a technique. She also had to learn that any effort a person puts in must be invested properly. But the most difficult thing was getting her to accept that her strategies were not effective. After all, they had always worked for her!

Claire had a hard time changing her study habits, but when her grades started to get better, she was back to having fun. Today, she's convinced that the change was worth it.

Claire is currently studying medicine. Although the first year is extremely hard, she is doing very well.

Claire

Whether your case is similar to Pablo's or Claire's,
or to neither, learning to learn will give you
an unexpected advantage.
Let's find out what that advantage is!

CHAPTER 1

In order to learn... RELATE!

Although we normally use the expression memorizing to refer to learning without understanding, we scientists call memory the ability that the brain has to generate recollections or to learn anything, from new knowledge to a new skill.

Memory happens because of the brain's plasticity, that is, the ability that this organ has to change its structure based on our experiences and actions. Thanks to this, the brain allows us to perceive, remember, understand, and do things in a way that we couldn't before. Every time you learn something, your brain changes!

A MOST PECULIAR MEMORY

The first thing you need to know to learn more effectively is that your brain does not work like a computer's hard drive. Why? Well, among other reasons, its ability to store information depends on the content of that information. You cannot learn everything with the same ease. To store new knowledge, your brain must be able to relate it to something you already know.

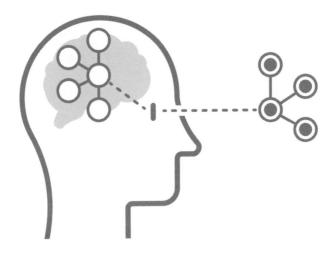

To store new knowledge, your brain needs to relate it to something you already know.

For example, imagine that I am just back from my vacation and I tell you that I've been traveling around the following cities. Read them once, close your eyes, and try to recall them (it doesn't matter the order).

Los Angeles
Chicago
New York
London
Paris
Rome

Now imagine that I visited these other cities. Do the same as before: read them only once and try to recall them.

Ngerulmud
Naypyitaw
Yamoussoukro
Honiara
Vientiane
Lilongwe

I'm sure it was much easier for you to remember the first list than the second one, although in both cases they are important cities. This is so because your brain finds it much easier to remember things that are related to something you already know. Computer hard drives, on the other hand, do not care about the information they receive because they store it without making any distinctions.

LEARNING MEANS CONNECTING KNOWLEDGE

The fact that it's easier for you to learn things when you can relate them to something you already know is a consequence of how human memory works: when the brain learns, it links the new knowledge to previously existing knowledge. But the brain can only do it if it notices that there is a connection between them.

That's why it is more difficult for you to learn things that are completely new to you, since you have barely any knowledge you can link the new information to.

For the same reason, the more you know about something, the easier it is for you to learn new things about it. That's because you have more knowledge that you can link to the new information. This way, you can retain this new information more effectively in your memory.

As a result, your ability to learn increases as you learn new things. But this happens only if you learn them well. And when you are trying to do this, good learning strategies can help you a lot.

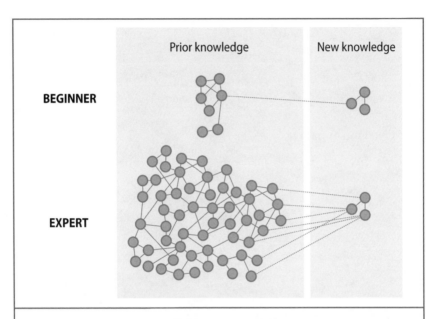

Prior knowledge · New knowledge

BEGINNER

EXPERT

We can interpret memory as a very large network of elements connected to each other. Your brain makes connections between memories and knowledge that are related. The more knowledge you have about something, the more connections you can make with new information related to it. This way, it is easier for you to learn.

As you can see, when you are learning something that's completely new to you, it's only natural that you find it hard to learn at first. You don't have much knowledge related to what you are learning as yet, so the first connections you make are few and far between. Also, it is likely that at first you use knowledge that is distantly related to the new information. In any case, you can learn only by making connections that are based on what you already know.

Core knowledge

You're probably wondering: if we need to build on prior knowledge to learn new things, how did we learn for the first time? Well, the answer is simple.

Before we are born, we all have some initial knowledge about the nature of objects, space, and living beings . This knowledge lets us organize everything that we will later learn through experience.

We use this nuclear knowledge, which is very basic, to build a large network of knowledge that comes from our experiences and actions. Therefore, most of what we know is the result of our experience. That's why we all know more about some things and less about others. This said, however, it's easy to change that: by learning more.

ACTIVATING YOUR PRIOR KNOWLEDGE

Sometimes you may have a hard time learning something because you still have little knowledge to connect it with. However, other times you have that knowledge but you're simply unaware of it. For example, read the following text and try to remember as much of it as you can.

First of all, you must get the height right. If you don't, it may be too challenging. Stability is key to making it work and not putting yourself at risk. Some people may need a little help at the start, but we all get it right in the end. Always try to allow yourself some space. Don't do it too quickly but not too slowly either, because in both cases you risk falling down. When you're done, you will need to lock it in a safe place or you may be in for a nasty surprise.

You may not remember many details in the text because it doesn't seem to make much sense. In other words, you don't know what prior knowledge to connect it with. But wait! What if I told you now that the text has the title "Riding a bike"? After knowing this, I'm sure you will get to remember many more things if you read it again. That's because you will link the text to what you already know about riding a bike.

So, to remember what you learn, you need to activate the knowledge you have that is most closely related to what you are learning. It is not enough to have that knowledge. You must also realize that you have it!

HOW DO YOU MAKE CONNECTIONS?

With everything you've read so far, you should already be getting an idea of some things you can do to learn better. That's right, to consolidate what you are learning, you must connect it to as much prior knowledge as possible.

That's all very good, but you must be asking yourself... How can I do that? How can we create links between what we learn and what we already know? To explain it to you, I would like you to do the following activity. I'm pretty sure it will surprise you.

Activity

First off, grab a pen and paper. Ready? OK, on the next page you'll find a two-column table with words in all the cells. Wait, don't look at it yet. I want you to do this first: read the words one by one, from left to right and top to bottom. Whenever you read a word from the column to the left, quickly count how many vowels it has and write the number on the paper. Then read the word to the right of that word and rate it from 0 to 10 depending on how much you like the meaning of that word (0 if you hate it and 10 if you love it). Write down the score on the paper. Follow the same procedure with the remaining words at the rate of one word every two seconds (not longer!), always from left to right and counting the vowels of the words to the left and deciding how much you like the words to the right. When you're done, turn over the page. So, are you ready? Then off you go!

T-shirt	Summer
Stoplight	Horse
Painting	Rain
Room	Bicycle
Tortoise	Smile
Championship	Sleep
Game	Knife
Lamp	Pizza
Pen	Swimming pool
Vegetable	Night
Flask	Field
Lipstick	Chocolate
Light	Book
Bubble	Tomato
Radio	Sand

All right, now turn over the paper you wrote the numbers on and write down all the words you remember from the table in any order. Come on!

Once you've written down all the words you can remember, go over the table again and check what column the words you have remembered are in. If you did the exercise correctly, you are likely to have remembered more words from the right column than from the left column. If that's not the case, I can still assure you that that's what happens most times.

Why is this happening? It's simple: what you did with the words in the left column did not lead you to think about their meaning (at least not on purpose). But when you worked with the words on the right, you had to focus on their meaning.

The best way to connect what you know with what you learn is by trying to make sense of it. When you think about the meaning of something, that is, when you try to understand what it means, you interpret it based on your prior knowledge. To decide whether you liked the meaning of a word, you thought about things related to that word, right? When you did that, you established connections with your prior knowledge.

REPETITION VS. ELABORATION

You may think that one of the best ways to learn is through repetition. Indeed, motor skills (such as dancing or shooting a basketball) require a lot of repetition to get better at them. But when it comes to acquiring knowledge, the question is: what should you repeat?

Saying or reading a word or phrase over and over is useless unless you think about its meaning. What happens when you try to keep a phone number in your mind in this way? You'll remember it long enough to dial it, but then you'll forget it right away. If you want the number to stick, it is better to look for familiar patterns in it, such as a date or a fact that you know. In other words, it's better to reflect on it. Much in the same way, copying a text without reflecting on its meaning is a pointless effort.

Thinking brings about learning

Thinking about what you learn is much more effective than merely repeating it. The following exercise is a good example:

Draw a $1 bill from memory

How many times have you seen one of these bills? Do you think you could make a detailed drawing of it?
You've probably seen it countless times, but you've never really paid

---

attention to it. This means you have never thought carefully about its appearance. Having seen it many times doesn't mean that you'll remember what a bill looks like. However, if you analyze it, look for patterns, think about the meaning of the images on it, or ask yourself questions about the reason for its design, you'll do a much better job of drawing its details from memory.

When you think about what you are learning and try to make sense of it, you learn it better.

This method of study, which consists of reflecting on what you are learning, is known as *elaboration*. We scientists felt that we should give it a name since it is hands down a more effective way of learning than mere repetition.

LEARNING STRATEGIES

To sum up, we learn best when we reflect on the meaning of what we are learning: when we make sense of it, when we try to understand it. By doing so, we promote the connection between our prior knowledge and what we are learning. This is what elaboration is about, and it includes the following strategies:

Start by getting a general idea of what you will study.

* Begin each study session by taking a look at everything you plan to study. Check the headings of the sections and the highlighted terms or names to get an initial idea of what it will be about. If you can write up a brief outline, all  the better. This way, you will begin to activate your prior knowledge that is related to what you will learn.

* Use the information you extracted from the brief analysis above to plan your study session based on the amount of time you wish to devote to it. Now you're ready to start!

While reading, take breaks and explain to yourself what you have just read.

- Make sure you understand what you are reading every few paragraphs. Do this by explaining to yourself what you have just read. It is not enough to have the feeling that you've got it. When you say it in your own words, it gets more firmly embedded in your memory!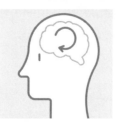

- If there is something you don't understand, don't be shy. Ask your teacher or someone who can help you. It is only normal that you do not understand something that is new to you. That's why you are learning! And if a classmate gets it right the first time, that is simply because he was lucky to have some prior knowledge that helped him. Get it yourself and you will be in the same boat!

When you try to understand something complex, think about other things that may be similar.

- For example, to understand what density is (the amount of matter per unit of space) you can think of a bus with different numbers of people in it. These comparisons, called analogies, will never be perfect. But they can help you in your first steps toward understanding something. When you see that a comparison you've used no longer fits well with what you're trying to represent, look for a better one!

- When you've come up with something that's similar to what you are learning, think about their similarities, but also about their differences. For example, arachnids look a lot like insects, but they are not the same. What are their similarities and differences? What do all arachnids have in common? What differences can there be between them?

Think about images that relate to what you are learning.

- One of the best ways to tie new knowledge to your memory is by picturing it in your mind. Whenever possible, use mental images and create visual stories about what you learn. You can draw them too, but don't waste time making a detailed drawing: the important thing is to know what these quick sketches come to represent!

Think of examples of what you are learning.

- Search your knowledge for specific examples related to what you are learning. If these things are related to your life, even better. For example, if you are learning about the structures that the Romans built to bring water to their cities, think about how you would do it or how we humans do it with today's technology. If you are studying a spelling rule, think of words that you know that meet this rule. If you are learning about a work of literature, think of everyday situations that remind you of its events.

Write a summary of what you understood in your own words.

- Writing a summary of what you have learned based on what you remember is a very effective way of making connections with your prior knowledge. But don't try to summarize many things at once. It is better to do several short summaries of a few ideas than one summary with a lot of information. You can also write short sentences with each of the ideas you have learned. But don't copy them from the original source! They must come out of your memory or it won't do you much good.

Create a concept map that includes the main ideas.

- A good alternative to summarizing is creating outlines in which you write down the concepts you have learned and connect them using arrows and comments to describe how they relate to each other. Indeed, this is what a concept map is all about. But don't do it thinking that someone will assess it. This map is only for you to tell yourself about what you have learned. If there's something that you do not remember, review it, but the most important thing is that you try to make the map without directly copying the information from the original source.

> **If you have to learn new vocabulary, think of similar words or expressions that you already know and relate them to each other.**

- This is a very specific strategy for situations like this one. For example, let's say you have a hard time remembering the word *silla*, which is Spanish for *chair*. In this case, you can try to associate this word to the expression *see ya!* Using this idiom as a cue, you will be able to remember *silla* because the Spanish word and the colloquial idiom in English sound very similar when pronounced. Also, if you associate this cue with an image or visualize it in a story, you will remember it much better. The more bizarre the cue, the more effective it will be. In this case, you can imagine you are saying goodbye to an old chair you are getting rid of!

If you have to remember a list of categories, objects, qualities, or processes, build words or phrases with them.

- This strategy is similar to the previous one, but this time you would use it to remember several words at once, especially if you need to remember them in a certain order. For example, if you are trying to learn the names and order of the planets in the Solar System starting nearest the Sun (Mercury, Venus, Earth, Mars, Jupiter, Saturn, Uranus, and Neptune), you can construct a cue such as *My Very Elegant Mother Just Served Us Noodles*. These techniques will be useful at first, but in time you will see how you can remember things without needing to use them—especially if you follow the tips in the chapters that follow.

My **V**ery **E**legant **M**other **J**ust **S**erved **U**s **N**oodles

My > *Mercury*   *Very* > *Venus*   *Elegant* > *Earth*   *Mother* > *Mars*

Just > *Jupiter*   *Served* > *Saturn*   *Us* > *Uranus*   *Noodles* > *Neptune*

These are just some of the strategies that will help you learn better because they are based on the way the brain incorporates new knowledge. However, other strategies based on other principles of the workings of the brain are even more effective. I have left them for the chapters that follow. I can assure you they are well worth knowing.

CHAPTER 2

In order to learn... REMEMBER!

Sometimes you may find it hard to learn something new. You put the work in, but you have a hard time understanding it or getting it right. However, your brain continues working when you have stopped thinking about it and readjusts its circuits so that you can do better the next time. The greater the mental effort you have made, the greater the changes that your brain will undergo to improve your performance. You learn more when you struggle!

Therefore, although learning something may be tough at first, this does not mean that you cannot master it. With dedication, your brain will reshape itself so that you can do it. Your brain is much more powerful than you realize.

SEARCHING IN YOUR MEMORY

As you've seen, your memory works in a very different way than the hard drive of a computer because it does not process all the information in the same way. Another important difference is that your memory does not have an index of all the memories and knowledge it stores. Besides, it cannot start a search that scans through all that information to find a specific piece of it. Your brain locates information in your memory by directly activating that which is related to what you experience. Therefore, if you read the words *capital of France*, it is very likely that the word *Paris* will instantly pop into your mind.

HAVING SOMETHING ON THE TIP OF YOUR TONGUE

But sometimes this system fails. I'm sure you have experienced that feeling of having something on the tip of your tongue: knowing that you know it but not being able to locate it in your memory. If someone says it before you remember it, you recognize it right away. Alternatively, you may also spontaneously remember it a little later. The thing is, it was already in your memory; you just couldn't get it to come out.

When you search your memory for something that you know is there but cannot bring it out into the open, what you usually do is think of things that you know are related to that piece of information, hoping that they will help you locate it. The clues that help you retrieve a memory or knowledge are precisely the prior knowledge that you connected it to when you learned it. That is why it is so important to make many connections: not only so that the new information is better tied to your memory, but mainly because it is much easier for you to locate it later. In other words, drawing many connections between what you know and what you are learning provides you with many possible paths through which to reach your precious knowledge when you need it.

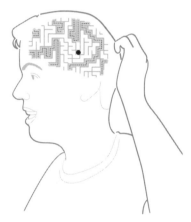

Let me highlight this important detail: it's one thing to have something in your memory and another to be able to find it. Both things must occur for learning to be effective. If one of them did not happen, you wouldn't be able to claim that you learned something. At least I don't think your teachers would be willing to accept that you knew something if you couldn't remember it at the time of the exam.

THREE LEARNING PROCESSES

To understand how your brain learns, it is important for you to know that learning necessarily involves three processes:

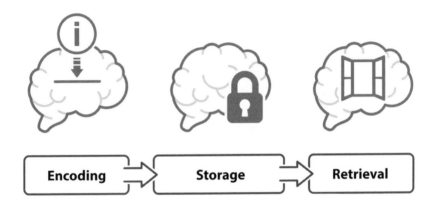

Encoding occurs when you focus on something and record it in your memory. Storage involves maintaining what you have learned for a length of time, which can be as long as a lifetime. Retrieval is the process by which you retrieve information that was stored in your memory. The latter is what happened when you remembered the capital of France, or what would happen if I asked you to tell me the fur colors of a panda bear. That image of a panda bear that you're picturing right now was stored in your memory, outside your consciousness, and you retrieved it to answer my question.

The fact that learning requires these three processes is much more important than you think. Keeping this in mind is key to understanding one of the most effective learning strategies.

RETRIEVAL PRACTICE

I mentioned before that your teachers would probably give you warm pats on the back if, during a test, you told them you knew something but couldn't find it in your memory. Now, if what you're asked to do in evaluation tests is to extract from your memory what you have learned, did you practice it before? Did you practice retrieval?

Suppose that in your test you need to put a ball through a hoop. How do you prepare for such a test? I guess by practicing shooting. So, why do most students spend most of their study time reading and rereading information (that is, encoding) rather than effectively practicing what they will be asked to do in the test, that is, retrieving it from memory?

I don't know if you are aware of what I am telling you here, but this is one of the most important keys to effective study: *retrieval practice*.

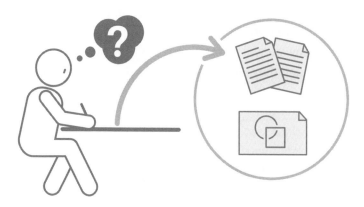

REPEATING ENCODING IS MISLEADING

Many students believe that learning consists of reading and rereading information, that is, repeating the encoding process several times. And the truth is that if you have a good memory, this system can be effective up to a point. But when the level of difficulty increases, this will clearly not be sufficient.

Also, practicing rereading only leads to very poor-quality learning. What you learn this way lasts only a few hours and it won't help you to continue learning later on. Remember that the more knowledge you get to embed in your memory, the easier it will be for you to learn other things related to this knowledge in the future. Therefore, although rereading may be useful right before an exam, it will hardly be of any other use after that. So, you can either spend that precious time of your life trying to simply pass the next exam or you can invest it in making things easier for you for later courses (not to mention the many other benefits that knowledge will bring you!).

What should be clear is that the reading and rereading strategy is misleading: it makes you think that it works better than it actually does. That's why many students do not understand why they didn't do well in an exam although they knew the material at home. This happens mainly for two reasons:

- First of all, since reading and rereading are effective in the very short term, it feels like you have mastered what you have learned right after studying it. But, of course, it's one thing to remember something today and another to remember it tomorrow.

- Secondly, reviewing by rereading the texts you have already studied gives you the pleasant but false feeling of knowing them well. But there's a difference between a text being familiar to you when you reread it and being able to retrieve it from your memory when you need it, without having it in front of you. To make retrieval easier, you must practice retrieval.

THE EFFECTIVENESS OF RETRIEVAL PRACTICE

Many scientific studies have shown that when we retrieve the information we have learned, we consolidate it more strongly in our memory, or at least we increase the chances of retrieving it again in the future. These studies have also found that this effect is much more efficient than repeating the encoding process (rereading).

The greater the effort we make to retrieve some information, the greater the impact it has on our memory. This is because our brain interprets this effort as an indication that what we are trying to retrieve is important for our survival. That's why it changes its structure to make retrieval easier the next time we need that knowledge.

A versatile strategy

Practicing retrieval is not only useful for learning specific information (e.g., the capitals of Europe) but is also very effective for learning all kinds of knowledge, especially concepts and procedures. Note that when you retrieve an idea, you must reconstruct it with your own words, and this strengthens the connection with your prior knowledge!

Without a doubt, rereading information is much more comfortable than having to retrieve it. You need to make a greater mental effort when you retrieve information, and it may also involve having to write down some questions to test yourself later. But the point is, if you spend the same amount of time with the two processes, retrieval will be much more effective than rereading. That extra mental effort that goes with it is what makes learning much more robust.

> **When you retrieve what you have learned, you consolidate it more strongly in your memory, or at least you increase the chances of retrieving it again in the future.**

THE OTHER BIG ADVANTAGE OF PRACTICING RETRIEVAL

Of course, many students use retrieval practice when they study, but they are usually unaware that doing so enhances their learning. Students tend to do it with a different purpose, which is nonetheless very important: to see if they remember what they have learned. In other words, these students realize that to make sure they know something, they must check that they are able to retrieve it from their memory.

Therefore, practicing retrieval is also beneficial because it allows you to detect weak points in your learning. Then, all you have to do is revise the parts that you did not manage to retrieve to reinforce them. Actually, it is very important to always check that the information you have retrieved is correct.

Retrieval practice, therefore, is nothing more than the practice of repeatedly evaluating yourself until the expected result is achieved. What's most interesting here is that your brain strengthens the knowledge learned every time you retrieve it: every time you evaluate yourself, you get to learn.

Finally, it is important to know that the effect of the retrieval practice is much greater if you allow what you've learned to be forgotten a bit. In other words, let some time pass between the time of study and the actual retrieval. But I will cover this in the next chapter. In it, I will tell you about another key method to improve your learning.

LEARNING STRATEGIES

The conclusion from this chapter is that we learn much more effectively when we try to retrieve what we have studied, that is, when we test ourselves and therefore force ourselves to retrieve what we have read, seen or heard from our memory. Studying in this way consolidates the knowledge we retrieve and, besides, it allows us to detect and go over what we do not remember well. This translates into the following strategies:

Review your notes using retrieval practice; don't reread them.

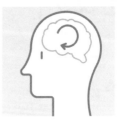

- Obviously, rereading is more tempting than retrieving because it requires less of a mental effort. However, it is also much less effective. And I'm sure you would rather not waste your precious time. So, whenever you review a lesson, start by trying to retrieve what you already studied. Go over the section titles or main concepts and tell yourself what you should know about them. You don't have to do it out loud or write it down if you don't want to: reviewing it mentally will be much better than not doing it at all.

Create recaps, concept maps, and more, but from memory!

- Creating recaps, drawings, or concept maps is useful because it allows you to think about what you are learning. It is also good retrieval practice, as long as you do it for reviewing purposes and without continually checking your textbook or notes. Actually, copying a text is one of the least effective ways to consolidating information in your memory. Retrieving it after having read it, on the other hand, is much more effective. In any case, make sure that the recaps or diagrams you have made are accurate.

Explain what you have learned to someone.

- A fun way of using retrieval practice is to explain the things you have learned to someone. If that person can ask you questions about it, even better. Indeed, one of the most effective ways of consolidating your learning is by teaching other people, as if you were a teacher. So, if a colleague is struggling, think that by helping them you will also be helping yourself since you will be enhancing your knowledge in the best possible way.

Write down questions to test yourself.

- As you study, write down questions that you can use later to practice retrieval. It's also worth writing down the answers to those questions or highlighting them in your notes to find them quickly when you need to review them looking for feedback. One way to do this is by creating flashcards: cards that have a cue on the front side and the corresponding answer on the other side. Today, there are many free applications to create digital flashcards.

Review your answers after practicing retrieval.

- Always check that the information you retrieved is correct. Sometimes, our memory gets confused and we are not aware of it. So, if you don't check your answers for accuracy, you might be consolidating the wrong sort of knowledge. This is not irreversible, but the sooner you correct it, the better. In that respect, flashcards will be useful to quickly check for accuracy.

Identify your weak spots and review them.

- In addition to boosting what you have learned by simply reactivating it in your memory, retrieval practice also tells you about what you still do not know well. Perhaps that's why, at first, it can be more frustrating than rereading: because it reveals the harsh truth. But don't be put off! After all, it is better to find out while you're studying than during the exam! So, make the best out of that information and go back over what you can't remember and what you find most challenging. You should practice retrieving that info until you get it right. Flashcards are also very useful for this type of practice because you can classify them according to whether you managed to answer them correctly or even according to how many times you had to use retrieval practice (over different retrieval sessions).

Do not resort to your notes or textbooks until you've really tried your hardest.

- When you try to recall something you have learned but you can't quite manage, do not throw in the towel just yet. Search for knowledge that is related to what you learned in your memory, like what you do when you have something "on the tip of your tongue." Before checking the full answer, you can look for cues in your flashcards or take a quick look at your notes for key terms to help you remember. If you are unable to retrieve it, you should know that your effort is still worthwhile: your brain will be more receptive to relearning that answer when you review it next in your notes.

Adjust the retrieval practice to the type of things you're learning.

- Retrieval practice is effective whether you want to learn specific data (e.g., new vocabulary, the capitals of South America, etc.) or ideas, concepts, or processes (e.g. photosynthesis, the hypotenuse, the causes of the Second World War, and so on). But you must adjust the practice accordingly. When it comes to facts or vocabulary, obviously you should retrieve them as is. But when it comes to more complex knowledge, which demands understanding, it is better to practice retrieval using your own words to explain the knowledge at hand. Don't recite definitions like a parrot! Your memory is much more effective at storing the meaning of things than storing a literal definition. Also, when you use your own words to describe a concept or procedure, you associate it more effectively with your prior knowledge.

Do not go back and check how you did an exercise. Instead, do it all over again!

- If your study involves procedural learning (math, physics or chemistry problems, grammar, and so on), don't just go over the exercises you did before: do them again! And don't start looking at the answers you completed before! You should only check them if you can't remember how to do the exercise or once you want to see how well you did. Obviously, it is a better idea if you try to solve new exercises, but it is important that you have some way of verifying how well you solved them.

Practicing retrieval is one of the most effective strategies you can follow to boost your learning. However, this can be done in a very specific way that makes it even more effective. I'll tell you about it in the next chapter.

CHAPTER 3

In order to learn... FORGET!

If you tell your brain to encode the same information over and over, as it does when you practice reading and rereading, it will encode it more fluently the next time you come across it. That is, you will be better at perceiving it. But if you tell your brain to retrieve it (to extract it from your memory), then it will do its best for you to retrieve it more efficiently the next time.

Actually, the harder you work on retrieving information from your memory, the stronger the signals you send to your brain telling it to make sure that info can be accessed more efficiently in the future.

AN UNSTABLE MEMORY

As we saw in previous chapters, science has revealed that our memory does not work in the same way as that of a computer. I already told you that the way the brain incorporates new information and the mechanisms it uses to retrieve it are very different from those of a hard drive. Well, in this chapter we will look at another important difference, this time related to the storage of information. Indeed, computers don't spontaneously "forget" information!

LEARNING AND FORGETTING

As soon as you learn something, you have already started to forget it. There's no question about it. However, the rate at which you forget things can be very different depending on how you learn them. We have seen this in the previous two chapters. But there is more to it. As you will see next, you can fight forgetting, and in doing so you will strengthen your learning. Believe it or not, to learn something more effectively, it is useful to allow your mind to forget it a little.

But... why do we forget? As we can conclude from previous chapters, there are two possible reasons behind us forgetting something: either because it is no longer in our memory, or because we are not able to find it. Although scientists still don't know exactly what happens when we forget, evidence points mostly to the latter reason: much of the forgetting happens because what we learned is still there in our brain but we cannot retrieve it.

We know this because it is much easier for us to learn something that we once knew (even if we are convinced that we have completely forgotten it) than to learn something for the first time. And the truth is that relearning something after having forgotten it consolidates it much more in our memory than restudying it when we still remember it.

SPACED PRACTICE

That's right! When you go over or practice something that you had totally or partially forgotten, you consolidate it more than if you review it immediately after learning it. Therefore, repeating a learning activity right after verifying that you've mastered it is not as effective as allowing periods of time between repeating sessions. Reviewing is most effective when you have started to forget some of it.

Therefore, it is much more effective to distribute the study and review sessions into several short sessions and space them out than to concentrate everything in a single long session. In other words, it is better to study something one hour a day for four days than to study it four hours in a row. Notice that I am not telling you to study more, but to distribute your study time in a way that will be much more efficient.

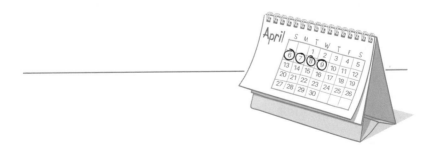

> **When you review or practice something
> that you had totally or partially forgotten,
> you consolidate it more than if you review it
> immediately after learning it.**

The strategy of breaking up the study sessions and allowing periods of time between them is known as spaced practice. Hundreds of scientific studies have shown that it's really effective.

As a consequence, repetition is effective for learning, but mainly when it is distributed. When you restudy after having included spaces between study sessions to allow some forgetting of what you've learned, you contribute to better consolidate learning.

THE WINNING COMBINATION

Spacing out the study sessions is positive in itself, regardless of the learning strategies you use in each session (including rereading). However, if you use these sessions for retrieval practice after the first session of elaborative studying, then you will have the winning combination. There is nothing more effective than spaced retrieval practice in tandem with elaboration.

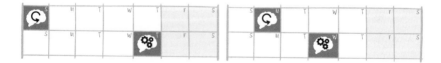

There is nothing more efficient than spaced retrieval practice combined with elaboration.

Remember that the greater the mental effort you must make to retrieve information from your memory, the more effective retrieval practice is. The brain is programmed to modify itself when you are engaged in an effortful task, thus making it easier for you the next time. And what better way is there to increase the challenge of retrieving some knowledge than allowing the mind to forget some of it? Spaced retrieval is the secret weapon of successful students!

THE KEY IS SCHEDULING

As you may have noticed, spaced practice requires something very important: that you plan your study sessions! Ideally, according to leading scientists in this field, you should be able to successfully retrieve what you learned up to three times, in three separate sessions. If you can't recall it, you must restudy it and start the count again.

This means that you should organize your study in such a way that you start each session by reviewing the previous sessions using retrieval practice, and then reinforce what you found most difficult to remember. Once you've done that, you can move on to the next topic.

You can space out your study sessions in several ways. The most effective is to distribute them over several days. If this is not possible, you can also do that over one afternoon. In this case, the best option is to use *interleaved practice*. According to this strategy, you should spend some time studying one subject and then some other studying a different one. After that, you go back to the first subject and review it using retrieval, and then you do the same with the second one.

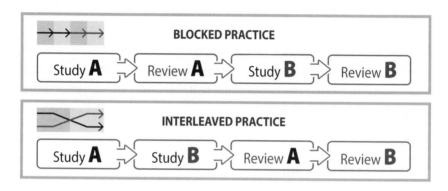

It is much more effective to interleave study and review in this way than studying and reviewing each topic as blocked practice. I know that your first reaction will be to question this, because if you review right after studying it feels as if you "know" the material better. But that's because you don't take into account the effects of forgetting. Interleaving, on the other hand, allows you to grapple with its effects, and the extra effort that goes with practice further reinforces your learning.

Some learning strategies make you feel as if you've learned more and better right after finishing studying, but that they are deceptive. The most effective strategies are those that are effortful and cause your brain to keep working once you're done, making changes so that next time it will take much less effort!

An inefficient strategy

Many students cram before an exam and still manage to do well. Indeed, studying right before an exam can be effective as long as you have a good memory.

Now, if this is the case for you, keep in mind that what you learn in this way won't stay with you for long. The time you devoted to it will have been wasted because you won't retain that knowledge and you won't be able to draw on it in the future. Also, even if this strategy of massed practice has worked for you so far, what will happen when what you have to study can no longer be crammed into a single study session before the exam? Using a single, long study session is a misuse of your time and a poor strategy when the topics of study become more challenging.

SPACING AND SLEEPING

As discussed before, spaced practice is most effective when you allow at least one day between each study session. This is so for two reasons:

- Because forgetting is greater and then retrieval practice will be more effortful, causing a greater impact on your memory.

- Because you can sleep in between sessions. And sleeping (especially sleeping well) is essential to consolidate learning.

Indeed, your brain uses the hours of sleep precisely to carry out the restructuring that was required from the learning activities. For this reason, sleeping helps you consolidate what you have learned.

Sleeping makes it less difficult for you to remember or understand what you were learning the day before. So, if after the last session you felt that you hadn't learned much because it was difficult for you to understand the study topics or you hardly managed to retrieve what you had learned when reviewing, you should know that the following day you will have a new brain with a greater capacity to do so.

Finally, scientists have discovered an interesting thing about spaced practice: the longer the spaces in between study sessions, the longer the information stays in our memory later. For example, reviewing what we studied once a week for five weeks makes us remember it for longer after the last session than reviewing it once a day for five days.

LEARNING STRATEGIES

In this chapter, you have seen that forgetting does not only work against you but can also be your ally. To make the best of it, you must organize your time of study in such a way that you can review what you have learned after you have forgotten some of it. This translates into the following strategies:

> ### Break up your study sessions into several shorter sessions.
>
> • If you use only a single session to study a topic and fail to review what you have learned later, it will have been a pointless effort. Being able to review is essential for learning. Doing it through retrieval is even better. And having time in between the study session and its review is second to none. Actually, the more review sessions you can do (spaced out in time), the more you will consolidate what you have learned.

It's best not to "overstudy."

- Sometimes, students keep practicing over and over something they have already mastered, or keep reviewing information they had already retrieved successfully during the same study session. We scientists call this "overstudying." In this respect, we strongly recommend practicing it again or retrieving the info after a while to allow some of it to be forgotten. Of course, if you can't find the time to review later, you'd better keep practicing for whatever time you have left.

Interleave your practice. (Part 1)

- A way to space out the practice within a short period of time (for example, over the afternoon) is to interleave your study practice by mixing different topics or subjects, even different types of problems. But always keep in mind that this allows you to separate in time the initial study of each topic from its review, while you focus on another topic. Of course, it is always better if you do the review using retrieval. (Remember that solving problems without checking the process by which to solve them until you have finished them is also an example of retrieval practice.)

monday

MAY
2

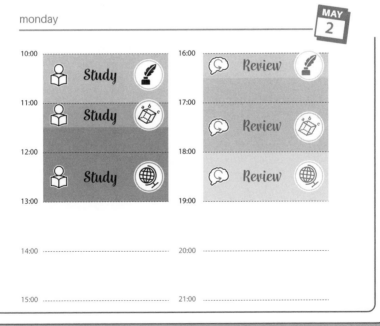

10:00		16:00	
	Study		Review
11:00		17:00	
	Study		Review
12:00		18:00	
	Study		Review
13:00		19:00	
14:00		20:00	
15:00		21:00	

Interleave your practice. (Part 2)

- You can also take advantage of interleaved practice if, after studying several types of problems or exercises, you solve them by mixing them randomly. However, it is very important that you do not know which part of the lesson each one comes from. Instead, try to infer it by reading the problem statements. In this way, you will avoid using the cues that tell you which part of the textbook they are in or what type of exercise you are about to solve since you won't be able to use those cues in the exam. This way of using interleaved practice is really effective.

Schedule your study sessions.

- Spaced practice is really effective, but to pull it off you need to organize yourself a little and make sure you do not leave everything to the last moment! Spaced practice does not require you to devote more time to study, but it does require you to use your time more intelligently. For example, it will be much more beneficial and easier to study a topic for half an hour over four days than to study it for two hours in a single day. Therefore, you must schedule a weekly (or longer-term) work plan.

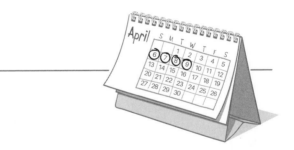

Keep your tasks up to date.

- When teachers suggest you do certain tasks, they don't do it to annoy you. They do it because they know that it is important that you keep practicing what you learn throughout the lesson, and they try to help you not to leave everything to the last moment. That is why it is key that you keep your tasks up to date. Besides, these activities will also help you follow the thread of the following classes more easily.

Review your study through retrieval practice.

- In the previous chapter, I told you that retrieval practice greatly increases your ability to remember what you learn. Spaced practice is beneficial whichever way you choose to review what you studied, but using retrieval practice is the best possible option.

Sleep!

- When you can sleep soundly between study and review sessions because you have distributed them over several days, the effect of spaced practice is optimal. In fact, not getting enough sleep the night before a test is usually not a good idea. Your brain needs to rest to be able to work properly the next day, and sleep is essential so that it can organize and firmly embed what you learned. While you sleep, the brain consolidates what it has learned!

TIPS FOR STUDENTS IN HIGHER EDUCATION

What if at some point you have to study a subject that is so broad it can't be covered in a few hours or even a few days? (This is often the case in higher education.) The key is to plan your study based on the principles described here. In this case, I recommend that you follow these steps:

> Organize the content by categories and divide it into units that you can study in sessions of about half an hour. It will be useful to create a list of topics based on this standard.

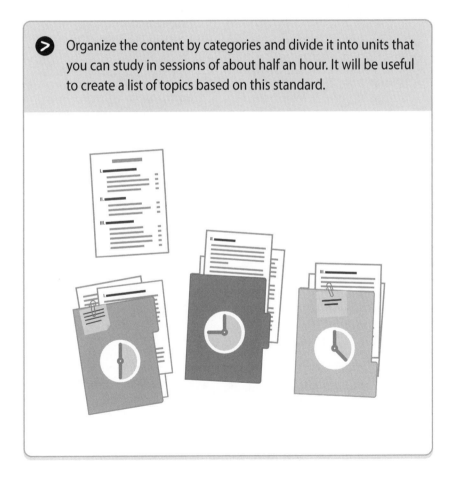

> Make an initial plan that includes one study session and at least three review sessions (using retrieval!) for each unit. Make sure you gradually allow more time between one review session and the next.

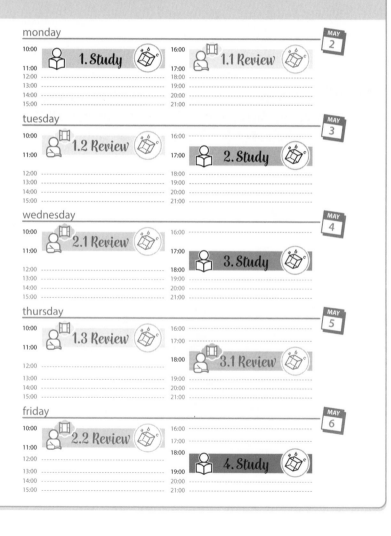

monday — MAY 2

10:00 / 11:00 **1. Study**

16:00 / 17:00 **1.1 Review**

tuesday — MAY 3

10:00 / 11:00 **1.2 Review**

16:00 / 17:00 **2. Study**

wednesday — MAY 4

10:00 / 11:00 **2.1 Review**

17:00 / 18:00 **3. Study**

thursday — MAY 5

10:00 / 11:00 **1.3 Review**

18:00 **3.1 Review**

friday — MAY 6

10:00 / 11:00 **2.2 Review**

19:00 **4. Study**

> Keep in mind that your initial plan may change. This is because it is worth adjusting the number of reviews of each unit and the spacing between them according to the difficulties you run into. In this respect, it is a good idea to classify the study units as you do them, depending on whether it was easy for you to recall them or not. If some units were difficult, review them after a short while (the next day, for example) until you get them without too much trouble. Then you should allow a longer period of time between the reviews of these units, and you can start studying other units in the meantime. If you find it difficult to retrieve the information of a unit (or a part of it) in the next review, make the period between reviews shorter again; if not, space them out even more. Keep adjusting the timing of the reviews and interweaving of units until you have retrieved the info you are learning from each unit up to three times without much difficulty.

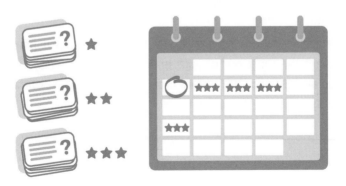

> ❯ Don't retrieve the same info many times within the same session (do not "overstudy"). It is better to defer the repetition, especially if you have already done it correctly. Take the time to review other units or study new topics instead.

Combining elaboration, interleaving, and spaced retrieval practice will help you get the most out of your brain. However, there are still other things to consider in order for your brain to realize its full potential. I will tell you about them in the next chapter.

CHAPTER 4

In order to learn... FOCUS!

If you want new knowledge to consolidate in your memory so you can have access to it whenever you need it, it is key that you reflect on its meaning and practice retrieving it. For example, you might use it to solve a problem. In any case, you won't be able to do any of this if you do not acquire this knowledge first!

To acquire new knowledge, information from your environment must reach your brain through the sense organs. But that is not enough. Your senses constantly receive much information that you never get to perceive; that is, you are unaware of it! For example, right now you may not feel the pressure that the back of your seat exerts on your back. But now you do, after I mentioned it.

For information to be learned, it must first be perceived. However, your brain can only handle a small part of all the information it receives at any given time.

WORKING MEMORY

In some respects, your brain does resemble a computer. For example, both have a type of memory that is used to hold a limited amount of information while operating with it. In computers, we call this the *Random Access Memory* (RAM), and in the brain it's *working memory*: the mental space where those things you focus on and pay attention to are represented. In short, we could say that it is the conscious part of your mind.

Working memory is filled with the information that you are perceiving right now from your environment through any of your senses, but also with information from your memories and knowledge, that is, information that is stored in your long-term memory. Thus, when you retrieve a memory or piece of knowledge, you carry it from your long-term memory to your working memory. In this way, you place it on the conscious plane of your mind. For example, if I ask you to think of an elephant, an image of an elephant that was in your long-term memory is activated and introduced in your working memory.

THE "PLACE" WHERE LEARNING OCCURS

Working memory not only allows you to mentally hold information temporarily but also to manipulate it. For example, I'm sure it's easy for you to imagine the elephant from before balancing on top of a ball and wearing a sombrero.

You are also manipulating information with your working memory when you try to solve a problem, that is, when you reason out. In fact, the little voice that speaks to you internally (and that is now reading these words to you) is part of your working memory.

Indeed, working memory is the mechanism that allows you to remember, imagine, and reason. Besides, it is the mental space where you create associations between your knowledge and the new information you receive. And as you know, these connections are critical if learning is to occur. Everything you learn consciously must first go through your working memory! Working memory is the prelude to long-term memory.

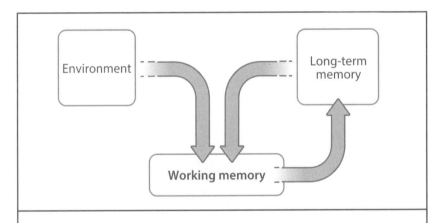

Working memory receives information from both the environment and long-term memory. If information from the environment is to reach your long-term memory, it must first pass through working memory.

> ### Learning while you sleep
>
> *The belief that you can learn by listening to a lesson through your headphones while you sleep is false. If the information does not pass through your working memory, which only happens if you are aware of it, don't count on it reaching your long-term memory.*

A LIMITED RESOURCE

If all the information you want to learn must pass through working memory, you must bear in mind that working memory has a very limited capacity! That is, it can only handle a small amount of information at any one time. This turns working memory into a bottleneck that restricts your efforts to learn.

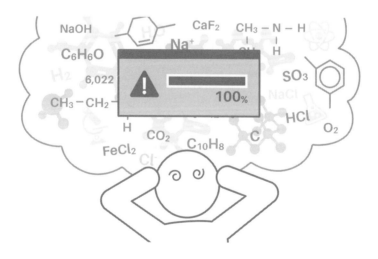

You can easily see how limited your working memory is if you try to memorize an increasingly long sequence of numbers. For example, if you try to hold this sequence in your working memory after reading it only once, you won't probably break a sweat: 4275. But it's a completely different story if you try to do it with this other sequence: 273981654328. You can also feel the limits of your working memory when you manipulate information. For example, it may not be very difficult for you to mentally calculate this operation: 4×13. But it is quite unlikely that you can solve this one in your head: 37×961.

If you tried to calculate the second operation without using a pen and paper, you've probably felt the unpleasant sensation of having your working memory saturated. When that happens, you can no longer advance and you empty your working memory at once, which forces you to start over with whatever you were trying to do. Therefore, it is very important to keep the burden of working memory at bay while you study.

COGNITIVE LOAD

Any information that makes its way into working memory will consume part of its resources. In other words, it will produce a "cognitive load." Therefore, it is key to differentiate between the two types of cognitive load that can occur when you study:

- **Relevant cognitive load.** It is produced by the information that you are trying to learn, as well as the mental operations that you do with that information.

- **Extraneous cognitive load.** It is caused by the information that accesses your working memory but is not related to what you want to learn.

Therefore, the extraneous cognitive load is everything that you can consider a distraction. It can come from both the environment (like surrounding noise) and your long-term memory (like when thoughts that are not directly related to what you are trying to learn keep coming into your head).

When you experience extraneous cognitive load, you have fewer resources to devote to the relevant load. Therefore you are squandering some of the potential your working memory has to learn. These resources are especially important when what you are learning is new to you or complex.

Working memory can't be trained

Working memory is not like a muscle that can be exercised to make it stronger. In other words, its capacity won't increase even if you regularly subject it to a lot of cognitive load.

In fact, the only way to optimize working memory when you learn something is to get some solid knowledge about it. The things you already know about what you are learning take up fewer working memory resources, leaving space for data and ideas that are new to you.

ATTENTION

Since the capacity of our working memory is very limited, it is key to control the information that occupies it while you study. Attention is precisely the mechanism that allows you to select the information that enters working memory and is kept there at any given time.

Unfortunately, attention does not work completely at will (and neither does memory!). You cannot choose not to pay attention to those stimuli in the environment that stand out, such as noise, moving objects, smells, and so on. If people could do this, we would most likely be an extinct species by now! However, although this keeps disasters at bay, it also makes studying more difficult. On top of that, it is not easy to avoid thinking about things that are unrelated to what you are studying, especially if you are tired or if you would rather be doing something else.

Although your attentional capacity can deal with all kinds of distractions and keep the focus on what you want, it is important to bear in mind that ignoring the many stimuli reaching you, as well as unwelcome thoughts, comes with a price: it produces mental fatigue. This is evident, for example, when you sigh in relief after a nagging noise in the background stops, even if you had succeeded in ignoring it until then. The more distractions you must ignore, the sooner you deplete your mental resources.

With all this in mind, it's highly recommended that you try to remove all elements that can distract you from your study environment. This is especially important for those that you know you are very distracted by, such as the phone or TV. Also, think about whether it is really necessary to listen to music or not.

STUDYING WITH MUSIC

If you like to study with music, take into account that music in the environment generates some extraneous cognitive load because it is a sensory stimulus unrelated to what you are studying. That is why it is very important that you identify why you do it:

- Some students use music to counter the noise in their study environment. If you can't remove the noise from your study environment and don't have earplugs, then music can help. Despite being a distraction, music that is familiar can be ignored more easily than unpredictable background noises, especially if they include voices. In this case, music is the "least bad" distraction.

- Some students find it really hard to pay attention to the task at hand, even when in silence, because their mind wanders off all too easily. For them, music can also act as a preferable distraction since it helps them to cover up one distraction with another that is easier for them to ignore.

- Finally, some other students play music to make study time more bearable, that is, for self-motivation. Clearly, if the alternative to studying with music is not studying, doing it with music is better. But, in this case, there are better choices that will not take away from the time to study.

In any of these situations, music will be a distraction and, as such, will consume some of your mental resources. Therefore, it is better to study in silence whenever possible. If you use music, it is better to go for music that is instrumental (without lyrics) and preferably calm.

Doing two things simultaneously

You can't do two things at the same time because of working memory limitations. When you think you do, you are actually rapidly shifting your focus of attention from one thing to the other. And this comes with a price: you end up doing both things worse than if you did one first, and then the other.

For example, try counting from 1 to 20 and then from 20 to 1. Now try to alternate one thing and the other: 1, 20, 2, 19, etc. Which one took you longer? Now, suppose I ask you to solve an operation like 12 × 15 while you're reading the paper. Impossible, right?

There is only one situation in which you can do more than one thing at a time: when you have automated any of them. Automated tasks are the ones you have learned so well that you no longer even need to think about them to do them. This means they no longer take up space in your working memory. That is why it is useful to automate processes such as solving multiplication tables, for example.

TO BETTER FOCUS YOUR ATTENTION, BE DISTRACTED!

The lesson from all of this is that, when you study, it is most effective to concentrate as much as you can on what you are doing. However, to stay focused, especially when you struggle with understanding something, it is beneficial to take breaks from time to time to rest mentally. During these breaks, your brain has a chance to better organize the information and "recharge its batteries." In this way, when you are back to focusing on the task, you will be better able to move forward with it.

That is why it is a good idea when scheduling your study sessions to include times when you can rest. You can also reward yourself during these breaks by doing things that you like, such as listening to music.

LEARNING STRATEGIES

In this chapter, I have introduced you to working memory: the mental "space" that allows you to hold information and consciously manipulate it. Any information you want to learn must go through it before it reaches long-term memory, where it can finally be stored. Unfortunately, working memory is a limited resource because it can only handle a very small amount of information at once. Therefore, if you want to take advantage of its full potential while you study, it is highly recommended that you follow the following strategies:

Get rid of as many distractors as you can from your study environment. (Part 1)

- If possible, choose a quiet place to study where there is not much happening around you. Moving objects will attract your attention!

Get rid of as many distractors as you can from your study environment. (Part 2)

- It is preferable that you study in silence. But if you are one of those who need music to concentrate or use it to counter the background noise, listen to music that is both familiar and relaxing and, most of all, that has no singing in it (especially if it is in a language you understand).

- Switch your phone into airplane mode and then... put it away! It is better to turn off any other device you may have around you that is not being used to study and also keep it out of your reach.

- Ask your relatives or roommates not to bother you while you are studying (unless it is a matter of life or death, of course).

Schedule your study sessions. (Part 1)

- Schedule a study routine that combines study times and rest times within the same session. Obviously, rest times should be shorter than study periods. Also, it's key that you take your routine seriously (especially when it's time to go back to your study room!). To do this, it may be useful to use a timer. The best option is a real timer, like the one in the picture. But if you don't have one, you can set multiple alarms in a row on your cell phone. In any case, keep it on airplane mode and in a place where you won't see it while studying.

Schedule your study sessions. (Part 2)

- Use the rest periods to unwind and do things that relax you and that do not involve a lot of concentration: listening to music, chatting, going for a stroll, dancing, checking your social media accounts, etc. In other words, give yourself rewards for the effort you have put in and will continue to put in.

Schedule your study sessions. (Part 3)

- If you like to play music when you study to make the effort more bearable, I strongly recommend that you listen to it during the rest periods and not put any on while you study. Also, use the breaks to do those things that you feel like doing and recharge your batteries to continue studying for a little longer. In this way, your effort will be much more efficient. Remember that trying to do two things at once is a waste of time: you can't take full advantage of the study and you can't enjoy the music fully, either. This is also true for any other distractions you try to combine with studying.

Ration your learning. (Part 1)

- The things that you have already learned well take up fewer working memory resources, leaving room for data and ideas that are new to you. Therefore, if you are studying something rather complex, it is very important that you plan your study to progress gradually, starting with the simplest concepts and moving toward the more elaborate ones. Remember how important sleep is for the brain to consolidate what it has learned, so try to distribute the learning objectives over several days.

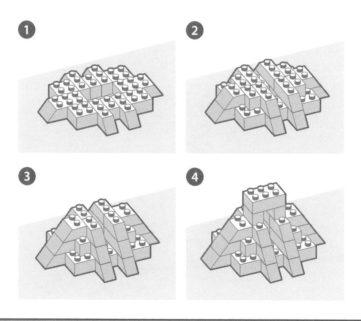

Ration your learning. (Part 2)

- If you are learning a new procedure, such as how to solve a mathematical problem or formulate chemical compounds, write down all the steps you follow. Doing this frees up resources in your working memory! If you don't believe me, look at how hard it would be to mentally solve a mathematical operation like 187×56, and then compare it to how easy it would be to do it using pen and paper. This is because as you progress with the operation, you need to hold more and more information in your working memory, information you are storing to perform the final steps of the operation but that you do not need during the intermediate steps. That's why writing down each step makes things easier for you.

$$
\begin{array}{r}
187 \\
\times\ 56 \\
\hline
1122 \\
+\ 935 \\
\hline
10,472
\end{array}
$$

1st
2nd
3rd

Ration your learning. (Part 3)

- Using graphic or even manipulative representations (physical objects) of what you are trying to learn is also very helpful because it reduces the amount of information that you must hold and manipulate in working memory. So whenever you can, lean on external resources to reduce the cognitive load.

Ration your learning. (Part 4)

- If you still think that you would rather "exercise" your working memory to "reinforce" it than do the things I have recommended so far, don't forget that the capacity of working memory cannot be increased. No matter how hard you try to "exercise" it by pushing it to the limit, you will achieve nothing. On the contrary, you will be wasting resources that you could devote to improving your learning, since working memory is where connections are made between what you learn and what you already know. On the other hand, although working memory cannot be increased, you can use it more effectively if you obtain solid knowledge and automate certain tasks: what you have learned well hardly takes up any space in the working memory when you need it.

Use different learning channels.

- Working memory can manipulate different kinds of information, especially visual and auditory information. But the most interesting thing is that it has independent "compartments" for each type of information. This means that if you simultaneously use both channels (visual and auditory) to learn, then you can get more out of working memory capacity. Therefore, whenever possible, look for visual representations of what you are learning that complement the texts, such as charts, animations, and videos. By the way, although texts access our minds through the visual channel, we expert readers have automated their conversion to auditory information: that little voice that reads the words in your working memory.

Now that you know everything you can do to make the time and effort you spend learning more productive, I only have to explain a couple of things that are also very important for learning. Indeed, the first of them is something you cannot go without. It is the key to the next chapter.

CHAPTER 5

In order to learn... BELIEVE!

Did you know that the brain of someone who has suffered a brain injury can be reconfigured to fully or partially restore the affected functions? Through proper training, the person can regain some lost skills. Even in extreme cases, such as children who had to have a brain hemisphere (half of the brain) removed following a serious disease, it is possible to restore much of what has been lost.

Your brain is extraordinarily plastic. Its function is to adapt to circumstances and provide you with the knowledge and skills that the environment requires you to acquire in order to survive and thrive. Brain plasticity is what allows you to learn. Because learning is adapting.

Learning is your brain's superpower.

WANTING TO LEARN

In the previous chapters, you discovered the actions and circumstances that will make your efforts to learn more effective. However, there is one thing that is at least as important as knowing how to learn: wanting to do it. Indeed, as with everything else, motivation is key to learning.

But simply being motivated to learn isn't going to make your memory more effective. Motivation is key to learning because it supports the actions that lead to learning. In other words, motivation makes you devote more time, attention, and effort to learning tasks. Therefore, knowing how to motivate yourself to learn is part of the good student's repertoire of strategies.

BEING MOTIVATED TO LEARN

What does your motivation to learn something depend on? First of all, it is clear that the value you place on what you learn influences your desire to learn it. If what you are going to learn is of interest to you, then you will be more motivated to learn it. This interest can be genuine, like covering a topic that you like or when the teacher makes the lesson fascinating. It may also be an indirect interest, such as when you are interested in learning something because it will allow you to achieve other goals that are important to you, such as solving an everyday problem, getting into a university, or getting a job.

However, it may surprise you to know that interest is not the most important thing for motivation. There is another factor that is even more relevant when it comes to being motivated to learn something: believing in your ability to learn it. In other words, if you don't believe you are capable of learning something, you will hardly make the necessary effort to achieve it and will end up losing interest in it. To learn something, you must be confident that you can learn it.

To learn something, you must be confident that you can learn it.

WE CAN ALL LEARN ABOUT ANYTHING

The good news is that our brains can learn about anything, be it math, science, or a new language, for example. Obviously, some will find it harder to learn things than others, and everyone will reach a different level. But, except for extreme cases, our brains can achieve remarkable levels of proficiency in any area if given the opportunity. It is about persevering and using the best strategies to learn, those that will make our efforts not be in vain. Indeed, these are the strategies that you have learned in this book.

However, most of us don't confide in our brains that much. We often think we are capable of learning some things but incapable of learning others. This happens because we mistake our initial ability with the fact that we can or cannot learn something. That is, when we struggle to learn something at the beginning, we assume we can never learn it and then become demotivated. On the other hand, when the opposite happens, that is, when we are initially good at something, then we convince ourselves that "it's our thing." And this way, we label ourselves (or get labelled) with that tag and settle for it.

LEARNING MINDSETS

Some scientists suggest that, faced with the challenge of learning something, we can adopt two types of mindset without realizing it. People who adopt a "fixed mindset" are those who believe that their ability to learn (or lack thereof) is an innate trait (from birth) and that it cannot be changed no matter how hard they study.

When these people perceive they're not good at something from the start, they don't think that their efforts can bear fruit and do not believe that good strategies can help them. Therefore, they choose not to show their supposed weaknesses: they don't give it a try or ask for help and refuse to answer questions (especially in public) by joking about it or making up all sorts of excuses. They believe that if they make a mistake, that will show they lack an ability. So they avoid taking risks and choose to save their reputation. At times, they may go as far as to sabotage their own efforts to learn so that they can give themselves the excuse of not having tried.

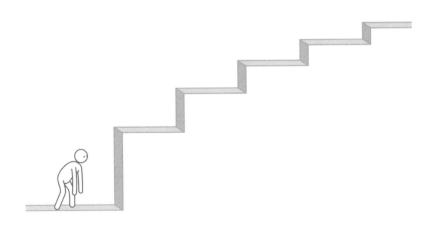

In contrast, people who adopt a "growth mindset" understand that difficulties and mistakes are part of the learning process. That is, they understand that it is normal to struggle with something at first, because they still have to learn it. Of course, they have a hard time when they fail, too. But what sets them apart from those with a "fixed mindset" is how they interpret failure: they don't see it as something definitive but as an indication of what they need to improve on. That's why they try harder; they are happy to seek help and persist in the face of adversity.

Here are some of the characteristics that define each type of mindset when faced with a specific learning challenge.

When a person adopts a fixed mindset, they...	When a person adopts a growth mindset, they....
Believe that their ability in an area of knowledge cannot be changed.	Believe that their skill in one area of knowledge is able to be changed.
Perceive mistakes as evidence of their inability to learn something.	See mistakes as something logical and necessary in the learning process.
Focus on saving their reputation.	Are focused on learning.
Get distracted during the learning task with doubts about whether they will be able to succeed.	Don't get distracted during the learning tasks with thoughts about their chances to succeed.
Don't take risks unless they can see a clear way to succeed.	Take risks, try, and put themselves to the test.
Get defensive in the face of challenges or criticisms.	Are motivated by challenges or criticism.
Are not willing to take responsibility for their mistakes and learn from them.	Are open to making mistakes and learning from them.
Give up as soon as they fail.	Persist after failing.
Believe that people who need to make an effort are not skilled enough.	Believe that, to be good at something, you have to work hard even if you have talent.
Feel threatened by people who stand out.	Are inspired by people who stand out.
Feel that seeking help is a sign of weakness.	Seek help to learn more and better.

A FIXED MINDSET AND GOOD GRADES

It is important to clarify that the "fixed mindset" is not necessarily that of students who struggle. In fact, most students who get good grades adopt this mentality: they believe that their ability to learn is something innate.

That's OK as long as things are going well for them. But when they don't, which usually happens in upper-level courses, this mindset makes it hard for them to seek help and believe they could improve by changing the way they learn. In fact, they interpret having to seek help as a sign of lack of an ability, just as they may believe that making an effort is only necessary if you're not skilled. Actually, many of these students try to hide the fact that they have to work hard to get good results.

It must be stressed that people are not differentiated by having one mindset or another. We all adopt both mindsets; it just depends on the skill we have at hand. For example, one can have a "growth mindset" for languages and yet have a "fixed mindset" for mathematics.

SKILLS ARE MALLEABLE

With respect to how the brain learns, science has shown us that the big difference between those who adopt a "fixed mindset" and those who adopt a "growth mindset" when faced with a challenge is that the former are wrong in their idea of learning. Thankfully, it is possible to change your mind.

As I have outlined before in this book, just because our brain is "wired" in a certain way does not mean that we cannot change it. Actually, that is precisely what learning is about: "rewiring" the brain to make us capable of doing things we couldn't do before.

Our innate (at birth) traits and past experiences determine how our brain is "wired." This gives us an initial advantage or disadvantage in learning each type of skill or knowledge. But in any case, the brain is incredibly plastic and is capable of modifying itself to achieve remarkable levels of performance in whatever it is we are trying to learn. Of course, this will take some time and effort. And so as not to give up right after the first try, you must understand that failing is part of the learning process, however painful it may be. We must also use effective learning strategies so that our effort is more likely to be rewarded. Trying too hard and failing is very demotivating. That is why you have to make an effective effort.

In any case, you must understand that effort and good strategies are not an absolute guarantee of achieving any learning goals. Effort is necessary to achieve your goals, and good strategies are a formidable help to achieve it. But other factors may cause you difficulty. Therefore, the help that you can get from other people and your own perseverance in the face of difficulty will play an essential role. Obviously, how much you want to persevere will depend on the value you place on your learning goals.

Do we only use a small part of our brain's potential?

I'm sure you have heard people say that we only use 10% of our brain's potential. However, this is not true. Our brain operates at full capacity, always working according to the circumstances. Even when we sleep, the brain is busy performing several tasks, such as reconfiguring its circuits to consolidate what was learned during the previous day.

If there is one potential use of the brain we may not be taking full advantage of, it is the brain's ability to learn. When we are not good at something, we believe that we will not be able to learn it. So, we give up. If we give up, we most definitely won't learn it. However, the brain is capable of this and many other extraordinary things. Of course, it needs time, opportunities, good learning strategies and ... perseverance!

REGULATING EMOTIONS

Whatever mindset we adopt when faced with a learning challenge, failures are never welcome. They produce negative emotions, such as sadness, shame, or anxiety, which we find very unpleasant. Knowing how to manage these emotions is key to not losing motivation.

Besides, emotions such as fear and anxiety come to the surface when we doubt our ability to overcome a learning challenge. If these emotions are very intense, they do not help us to achieve our goal—quite the opposite. Intense emotions hijack our working memory resources and alter our attentional capacity, which are key for learning and doing well on tests.

Although being too nervous during an exam or presentation is never a good thing, a moderate level of restlessness keeps us on our toes and improves our performance. That's why successful students use strategies to deal with their emotions and keep them at optimal levels, both before and during tests. Although, like with all other effective strategies, they often apply these strategies without knowing it.

One of the keys to these strategies is to adopt a "growth mindset," that is, to believe in our own ability to learn, to play down mistakes and failures, and to rely on good learning strategies.

LEARNING STRATEGIES

As you have seen in this chapter, knowing how your memory works and what you can do to unleash its full potential is important to achieving your learning goals, but it won't do you any good if you think that whatever you do, you won't be able to learn. What is the point, then, in knowing the learning strategies you've discovered in this book if you don't put them into practice? That's why you must take care of your own motivation and learn to regulate your emotions.

Here are some strategies and ideas to help you.

Believe in yourself.

- I know it's very easy to say that you have to believe in yourself, but it's not so easy to do. However, in this book I have told you many things about your brain that can help you do this. But I did not explain them to you to cheer you up. I am a scientist, and whether we like what the evidence reflects or not, it is my duty to share it. Thankfully, research on the brain brings us good news: we may find it more or less difficult, and we may all obtain different results, but the levels of competence we can all achieve in any area of knowledge are significant. Unfortunately, this is not the case with severe intellectual disorders, but we can all improve our skills with training and study. Even people with specific learning disabilities, such as dyslexia (a condition that makes it difficult to learn to read and write), can overcome them. Of course, people with learning problems may have to make much more effort than those who do not have them.

Don't attribute your successes and failures to fixed or uncontrollable causes. (Part 1)

- If you are good at studying, I won't deny that this ability is partly the reason for your academic achievements. However, it is only one advantage. What if someday this is not enough? You need to understand that blaming the teacher, the difficulty of the test, or anything else outside your control will be pointless (even if you are right). You shouldn't think that your innate ability has changed, either. If you want to overcome the situation and you are in a position to do so, try harder or, even better, go over your learning strategies. Keep in mind that sometimes more of the same effort won't help: you need to put in a smarter effort.

Don't attribute your successes and failures to fixed or uncontrollable causes. (Part 2)

- If you think that you're not cut out for studying, you should not attribute your failures to a supposed inability to learn. Your brain can handle that and much more. Rather, reflect on whether you studied enough and, above all, whether you used the most  effective strategies to learn. OK, I'll grant you that they are not a silver bullet, but if you use them and have faith in them, you will notice a major change.

- Keep in mind that one of the most relevant factors for learning is your prior knowledge, so allow yourself time to build the knowledge base that you will need to achieve goals that now seem unattainable.

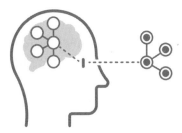

Interpret your mistakes and failures correctly.

- Nobody likes being wrong, but everyone is at some point. We make mistakes day in and day out, especially when we are learning something. That is why we are learning it, so that we won't do as badly the next time! But even the greatest ones in any given discipline, be it academic, artistic or in sports, make big mistakes. However, no matter how frustrated they may feel, they embrace their mistakes and learn from them to keep improving. For example, Michael Jordan, one of the best basketball players in history, put it like this:

  > "I have missed more than 9,000 shots in my career. I have lost almost 300 games. Up to 26 times I was trusted with the last, winning shot and I missed it. I have failed over and over again in my life. And that's why I have achieved success."

  By using this example, I don't mean to say that anyone can become the best in the world at whatever they choose to do, but that even the best in every field make many mistakes. Therefore, we should not interpret mistakes as a reflection of our supposed inability. Actually, the underlying message in this quotation is that we need to be able to overcome difficulties if we want to learn and improve in any field, as well as to accept mistakes and learn from them.

Think of talent as just another advantage. (Part 1)

- Just as we often misinterpret mistakes as evidence of our supposed inability, we also misinterpret talent. Having a talent for something does not mean that we are only capable of learning about that thing. Nor does it mean that we don't need to make an effort to learn it. It is only an advantage that we have in reaching our learning goals. Talent makes learning something less difficult at first, but it is not enough on its own to allow us to achieve higher learning goals. Without putting in work and effort, talent is of little use.

Think of talent as just another advantage. (Part 2)

- Not having a special talent for something when we set out to learn it doesn't mean that we can't learn it. The average expert in any field is a regular person who has studied or practiced a lot. However, we tend to ignore the time that it has taken them to achieve mastery of their disciplines. Even people who are very prominent in their professions have had to overcome great learning difficulties. For example, John Irving, who has won several literary awards and even an Oscar for best adapted screenplay, had to deal with dyslexia before becoming a successful writer.

Think of talent as just another advantage. (Part 3)

- Keep in mind that the ease of learning something is not only the result of your innate traits. It also depends on your prior knowledge! After all, you modify your brain as you learn. Therefore, the more you learn about something, the easier it is for you to learn new things about the same topic, or, in other words, the greater your talent for learning more about it.

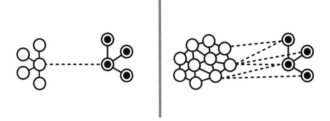

Note: In this book we have focused on learning that involves acquiring knowledge and developing "intellectual" skills, such as language, mathematics, and so on. In learning "motor" skills, such as dancing or sports, talents and limitations to achieve high levels of competence not only depend on the brain but are also determined by the physical characteristics of each individual.

Use techniques to regulate your emotions. (Part 1)

- One of the best ways to control the emotions that arise when faced with a learning challenge is to follow the directions above. Correctly interpreting the meaning of failure and believing in yourself is essential if you want to keep your emotions at bay. However, no matter how much I tell you to believe in yourself, and no matter how much I explain why it makes perfect sense for you to do so (because your brain can handle it), you will hardly begin to believe in yourself if you don't see improvements in your results.

- While motivation is important to reaching new learning goals, achieving them is even more important to motivation. Therefore, good learning strategies, which will help you get the most out of your effort, will be key to maintaining your motivation. But you must first find enough initial motivation to set them into motion. Getting started is up to you.

Use techniques to regulate your emotions. (Part 2)

- If you study using spaced retrieval practice, which actually is a way of making sure that you can remember or do what you learned, you will know if you are well prepared to face a test. Scientific studies show that studying using spaced retrieval helps us feel more confident and makes us less likely to blank out during exams.

- What if you feel too nervous before or during a test? Try to control your breathing, making it slow and deep. If you can, listen to relaxing music for a few minutes and picture a nice place in your mind. However, if you have serious problems with anxiety during tests, you should seek help from a specialist.

Use techniques to regulate your emotions. (Part 3)

- Another situation in which it is important to regulate your emotions is when you are studying and there is something within your reach that motivates you more. Overcoming those temptations when you know you should be studying is part of your ability to regulate your emotions. In the previous chapter, I mentioned two ways to help you do this: putting away objects that are reminders of what you would like to be doing (such as your cell phone) and organizing your study sessions so that you can take breaks in between to do what you like doing, such as listening to music, chatting with friends, or watching videos on YouTube. Remember, you can use a timer to help you stick to your planned schedules.

Learning is something that happens in your brain and is therefore ultimately up to you. Still, people around you—and not just your teachers—can help you learn better, and you can help them too. For this reason, in the next chapter, the last one, I will tell you about the important role that the interactions with your classmates play in achieving the learning goals that you share.

CHAPTER 6

In order to learn... COLLABORATE!

As you already know, your brain learns from each and every one of your experiences. Those experiences include interactions with other people, that is, social interactions. In fact, most of the things you learn every day come from situations that involve other human beings. Even when you think you are learning by yourself, like when you are reading a book, you are actually learning because someone shared their ideas and knowledge through writing.

The social interaction most clearly linked to learning is teaching. Actually, there are few ways to promote our learning as effective as having someone teach us. But even when we interact with other people in situations where the distinction between teacher and learner is not so clear, we also get to learn. Learning is mostly a social activity.

WE ARE MADE TO LEARN FROM ONE ANOTHER

Human beings are a social species. We organize ourselves in families and communities to cooperate and thus overcome all kinds of vital challenges that we couldn't overcome by ourselves. There are other examples of social species in nature, but none has been as successful as ours. One of the reasons is that the individuals of our species are not only capable of passing their genetic inheritance down to their descendants, but they can also give them their extensive knowledge. On this basis, each new generation can build on this knowledge and attain new wisdom.

Have you ever seen, say, a five-year-old teaching his friends how to do something? Teaching our peers (even other animals) is something we do naturally, from a very early age. In the same way, our brain also shows a clear predisposition to learn from individuals of our species.

In short, if one thing has allowed us to stand out as a species, it is our great ability to learn from the world around us, and especially from our fellow humans—and not only *from* them but also *with* them.

Animals with culture

Apart from humans, other social species in the animal world also show signs of cultural transfer across generations, although to a much lesser degree than the human species. This is the case of orcas, for example. Indeed, the families of orcas (also called killer whales) that live in different parts of the world have different hunting strategies. These are not written in their DNA; they have been passed from one generation to the next through social interaction.

Beyond the situation where a teacher teaches us, there are many reasons our interaction with other people (such as our classmates) can contribute to our learning, while at the same time we contribute to theirs.

LEARNING BY TEACHING

As I told you in the chapter on retrieval practice, one of the best ways to consolidate what you have learned is to try to teach it to other people. So, when you help a classmate who finds it hard to learn something, you also help yourself. And this is due to several reasons:

- Because when you teach someone what you have learned, you consolidate it in your memory by the simple fact of retrieving this information and explaining it in your own words.

- Because teaching something to another person, especially if they find it hard to understand, often forces you to try to express the same thing in different ways. This leads you to increase the connections with your previous knowledge.

- Because when you try to teach something so that it can be understood, you can become aware of inconsistencies or weaknesses in your knowledge.

- Because the people you teach can ask you questions that lead you to discover new insights in your knowledge.

Ultimately, few ways of consolidating and enhancing our learning are as effective as trying to teach other people. Plus, at the same time, you also help them. This is a good example of how cooperation contributes to the benefit of everyone.

Now, for this to happen it is not only important to be willing to help but to be open to receiving help when you need it. Indeed, sometimes you may find it hard to admit to not understanding something. You may worry about what others will think if you ask for help. But as we saw in the previous chapter, it is better to adopt a growth mindset and focus on learning, leaving aside concerns about appearances.

Learning begins as soon as we admit we do not know something. And that's not a big deal, because we can fix this by learning it.

However, there are other social situations that are also enriching for the learning of all the people involved, even if there is no one to act as a "teacher" for them. Let's see them below.

LEARNING THROUGH DISCUSSION

The conversations and especially the discussions that we have with other people are unique learning situations. When we exchange ideas with people who have knowledge and interests that differ from ours, we are enriched by their different perspectives. In fact, we are not often exposed to other points of view on certain topics because we usually prefer to surround ourselves with those who share our ideas. Indeed, we can learn by discussing, but what we learn will depend on whether we are open to the possibility of being wrong, which is not easy.

As you may remember, when we learn we build knowledge networks in our brain, linking what we know with new information. But when new information doesn't fit into our knowledge structures, then we experience a *cognitive dissonance*. For example, imagine someone saying this to you:

Time doesn't run at the same rate everywhere.

It's disconcerting to hear statements like this one because the concepts that we have built in our memory, as well as the relationships between them, are not compatible with what the new information tells us. And since remaking our knowledge structures is costly, the brain automatically prompts us to try to protect them.

This is when we show our confirmation bias: the tendency we all have to seek and remember information that matches our ideas and to ignore and forget information that does not fit with them.

For example, when someone questions something you know, you usually search the Internet for the information that proves you right. You never consider checking if that person might be right. In fact, if you come across any information that supports their position, you dismiss it or play it down and quickly forget about it. Ultimately, when we perceive that someone questions the validity of our knowledge, we feel attacked and the confirmation bias is a defensive response to this.

Defending our own ideas and knowledge in a discussion or conversation helps us to consolidate them. It forces us to structure them, give examples, make analogies, find more information to validate them, and so on. And this engages us emotionally with those ideas. Even so, a discussion is always much more enriching (and enjoyable) if we show open-mindedness and make the effort to try to understand the position of the person or people we are communicating with. When we do that, we can learn things that we would never have imagined.

In short, discussing ideas and issues with other people, especially if their concerns and knowledge are different from ours, gives us very different views of things and allows us to reflect on what we know.

Looking up information on the Internet

Remember that anyone can publish content on the Internet, so you must be careful with the information you find there. Always verify that the information comes from reliable sources, try to figure out why it was published, and check it against other trusted sources. And don't let your confirmation bias decide which sources are the most reliable!

LEARNING BY COOPERATING

Of course, interacting with people who share your interests is also beneficial for learning. Indeed, one of the things that can contribute the most to learning is that several people with a common goal work together to achieve it. For example, when we scientists collaborate to investigate a phenomenon or find a solution to a problem, it is precisely when we learn the most and, at the same time, it is when scientific knowledge advances the most. If we also cooperate with scientists from other disciplines, our horizons broaden enormously.

That's right: when it comes to achieving a goal, cooperation also benefits from the diversity of people participating in the same project. In turn, this diversity contributes to the learning of all those involved. But for cooperation to be successful, all team members must commit to achieving common goals and show their willingness to intervene and communicate in a transparent, proactive, and friendly manner.

LEARNING STRATEGIES

In this last chapter, I wanted to emphasize the relevance of social interactions in learning. After all, our brains have evolved in such a way that they have a talent for learning from our peers and also with them. Even if you prefer to study alone, you can still benefit from helping other people or from the help that they can offer you at any given time. When we learn together with other people, we explore ways of learning that are essential to our nature. And we all benefit.

Here are some tips to help you learn with and from others.

Engage in group retrieval practice. (Part 1)

- As I have pointed out a few times in this book, the easiest way to engage in retrieval practice with others is by explaining to them what you have learned. If you explain it to them in a way that they can easily understand and learn from, then your best efforts will translate into greater benefits for your learning and for the learning of the people you teach!

Engage in group retrieval practice. (Part 2)

- Using retrieval practice with others can also be understood as a form of group self-assessment. In this case, someone can be in charge of asking the questions while the others answer them, or you can all produce the answers in writing, compare them, discuss them, and agree on a final answer before reviewing the correct solution. Doing this reflective exercise will help you make better use of retrieval practice.

Engage in group retrieval practice. (Part 3)

- Using flashcards is a good way of assessing yourself, but sometimes you may not have enough time to create all the flashcards you need. But what if you worked as a team and prepared a lot of them together with some classmates?

- Remember that retrieval practice is used to review what you have learned after you've been studying a topic. Therefore, it is when you're reviewing that it makes the most sense to teach others or learn from them. Learning alongside others has its advantages, but you will also benefit from learning by yourself when it is most appropriate to do so (such as when you tackle a lesson for the first time or when you need to focus).

Seek help if you have difficulties.

- Don't be shy asking for help if you have difficulties understanding or learning something and can't figure it out on your own. Seek the support of a person who can teach you directly or who can tell you where to find that knowledge. If you refuse help simply to save your reputation, you run the risk of not meeting your learning goals.

Get involved in team discussions and tasks. (Part 1)

- As you have seen, discussions and teamwork activities are excellent opportunities to learn if you get actively involved in them. As for discussions, taking part in them can help you consolidate your knowledge, contrast it, or reflect on it. But it is important that you keep your confirmation bias in check and try to understand the perspectives of others without shutting down. By contrasting your ideas with those of others, you improve your learning, whether your ideas eventually change or not.

Get involved in team discussions and tasks. (Part 2)

- Remember that carrying out a task as a team is simply a way of helping each other to learn from one another, a practice that as you now know benefits everyone. A diversity of the team members helps everyone's learning. Keep in mind that the goal of the task is not to win a competition, but to learn as much as possible from this experience.

- Don't take your teammates for granted! You could be in for a surprise after finding out that they had knowledge or skills that you did not think they had.

At this point, I have told you about the keys that will help you maximize the effectiveness of your efforts to learn. It is all in your hands now. As for me, I can only insist that whether you are a student who is doing well or not, these strategies will give you a significant boost. This is supported by scientific research and also, for what it's worth, by my experience with dozens of students I have helped.

I wish you the best in all your endeavors, both in school and in light of any future challenges that may require you to learn something (and probably all of them will!). Thankfully, the human brain can learn throughout our entire life. Take advantage of it now that you know how to best do it!

Acknowledgments

A book is hardly ever the result of the work of a single person, and these pages are no exception. For this reason, I would like to express my gratitude to the people who have helped me through the process of creating it and who have been as enthusiastic about this project as I have been.

First and foremost, to Ariadna Álvarez, for her unconditional support at all times and also for her invaluable editing work, leading the design, illustration, and the team of translators and proofreaders. I also want to express my gratitude to Sandra Villa (designer and illustrator), Isabel Soler (illustrator), Oriol Sole (English translator), and Kirsti MacPherson (English proofreader). And last but not least, to Jordi Rabascall for his artful design of the cover in the original version of the book.

I also want to acknowledge Albert Romero for his valuable contribution. He has helped me improve my writing style and has given me great tips on how to make it more accessible to younger readers. In this sense, I also want to express a particular gratitude to Janna Vila and Pau Vila for acting as young editors and providing me with their invaluable opinion about the texts and the design of the book cover (with a little help from their mother, Begoña Sanz).

I would also like to express my gratitude to Sergi del Moral and Javier F. Panadero, two teachers I look up to, for their feedback. Their expert insights have helped me finish several aspects of this book.

And finally, I especially wish to thank my parents, not only because this book ultimately exists thanks to their efforts to provide me with the best education they could, but for all their support in everything I have done over the last (almost) 40 years.